Praise for Susanna Wright's new edition of
John Baillie's *A Diary of Private Prayer*

꽃

"This new edition of John Baillie's classic is a wonderful resource for anyone wishing to go deeper in their prayer life. I recommend this new edition to all who wish to see their daily prayer life expanded and blessed."

—**Mark Batterson**, *New York Times* bestselling author of *The Circle Maker*

"The adjective 'venerable' ought to be reserved for those classics that have stood the test of generations. John Baillie's *A Diary of Private Prayer* has surely earned this title. This classic of Christian spirituality has been in constant use since its publication in 1936. Thousands of men and women have found comfort, wisdom, and challenge in Baillie's prayers, rendered utterly without pretense. My own dog-eared copy of the *Diary* has been a companion since college days. But even the most ardent fan of this classic has longed for an edition that speaks with a fresh, contemporary voice, precisely the voice Baillie employed in his own time. We can be grateful to Susanna Wright for the respect with which she has handled Baillie's prayers and the reverence with which she ushers us into the presence of God. If it is ever proper to speak of a new classic— and one surely should do so only with great care—it is possible to speak of Wright's new edition of John Baillie's *Diary*."

—**Michael Jinkins**, president and professor of theology, Louisville Presbyterian Theological Seminary

"Since its initial publication . . . *A Diary of Private Prayer* has become established as a modern spiritual classic. Now translated into several languages, it has become the bestselling work of any Scottish theologian. The *Diary*'s breadth of subject matter, felicity of language, and simple piety have impressed its many readers at different times and in diverse circumstances. This updated edition admirably preserves all these qualities while ensuring that John Baillie's *Diary* will continue to be accessible to another generation."

—**David Fergusson**, professor of divinity and principal of New College, University of Edinburgh

"*A Diary of Private Prayer* by John Baillie sold over a million copies and blessed many Christians over the last century. This contemporary version will open it up to a new generation and will be a great aid to prayer for those starting out on their prayer lives, as well as to long-standing Christians."

—**Nicky Gumbel**, author, founder of Alpha International, and vicar of Holy Trinity Brompton, London

"When this book was first published almost one hundred years ago, it was quickly recognized as a classic of devotional writing, and I'm delighted that Susanna Wright is now making it available and accessible to a new generation of readers seeking resources to help them grow in prayer."

—**Pete Greig**, author of *God on Mute* and founder of 24-7 Prayer

"Prayer is the language of faith. Like any other language, the best way to learn it is to listen to native speakers and practice. In this book, the beginner will find ideas, words, and patterns that will help to guide and grow their own prayer life—and those who have been praying for longer will find fresh inspiration. But most importantly, all who use this book will draw closer to the God who came to speak to us in our language so that we may learn His."

—**Jane Williams**, theologian, author, and wife of former Archbishop of Canterbury Rowan Williams

"Susanna Wright has done contemporary Christians a great service by making John Baillie's classic available and accessible to a new generation. The prayers in this book will deepen, enrich, and transform anyone who prays them seriously."

—**Rev. Dr. Graham Tomlin**, dean of St. Mellitus College, London, and author of *The Provocative Church*

$\mathcal{A}$ Diary of Private Prayer

John Baillie

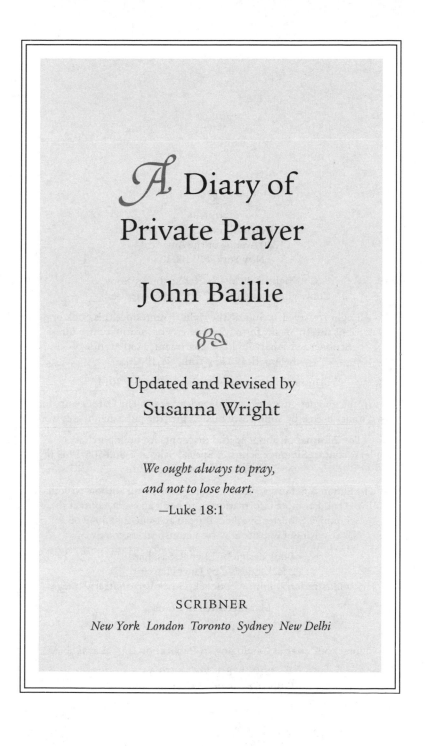

Updated and Revised by
Susanna Wright

*We ought always to pray,
and not to lose heart.*
—Luke 18:1

SCRIBNER
New York London Toronto Sydney New Delhi

SCRIBNER
A Division of Simon & Schuster, Inc.
1230 Avenue of the Americas
New York, NY 10020

This Scribner hardcover edition October 2014

SCRIBNER and design are registered trademarks of The Gale Group, Inc.,
used under license by Simon & Schuster, Inc., the publisher of this work.

For information about special discounts for bulk purchases,
please contact Simon & Schuster Special Sales at 1-866-506-1949 or
business@simonandschuster.com.

The Simon & Schuster Speakers Bureau can bring authors to your
live event. For more information or to book an event, contact the
Simon & Schuster Speakers Bureau at 1-866-248-3049 or
visit our website at www.simonspeakers.com.

Book design by Ellen R. Sasahara
Jacket design by Janet Hansen
Jacket illustration © John Woodcock/iStock Vectors/Getty Images

Manufactured in China

19 20 18

Library of Congress Cataloging-in-Publication Data is available.

ISBN 978-1-4767-5470-3
ISBN 978-1-4767-5471-0 (ebook)

For
I A N

Preface

For almost a century, John Baillie's extraordinary classic *A Diary of Private Prayer* has aided and inspired many readers into a deeper prayer walk with God. When I first discovered it, I was enthralled and challenged by the prayers, and it has since become a crucial resource for my prayer life.

I soon wanted to share this treasure with others, but found that the King James English style of the original seemed to prevent the prayers from being accessible for everyone. It is my hope that this new edition, composed in a more contemporary style, will open up the prayers for another generation, and that readers old and new alike may be blessed by the faithfulness and wisdom of John Baillie.

I am especially grateful to Baillie's son, Ian, to whom *A Diary of Private Prayer* is dedicated, for his support and for choosing me to undertake the updating of this classic book before his death in 2008. I am also very grateful to the Baillie family for their support in this venture and for putting me in touch with the Rev. Dr. Robin Boyd, himself an experienced religious writer, who worked with me on the project. Dr. Boyd was a student of John Baillie at New College, Edinburgh, and years later became a friend of Ian Baillie. Without his contributions of scholarly insight, wisdom, and patience, this new edition would not have been possible.

Susanna Wright

Author's Note

*H*ere are prayers for all the mornings and evenings of the months; and at the end of the book two prayers which, when any day falls on a Sunday, may be substituted for the others or else added to them. These prayers are to be regarded as aids; they are not intended to form the whole of the morning's or evening's devotions or to take the place of more individual prayers for oneself and others. On the blank left-hand pages such further petitions and intercessions may be noted down.

The prayers are suited to private use, not to the liturgical use of public worship.

—John Baillie

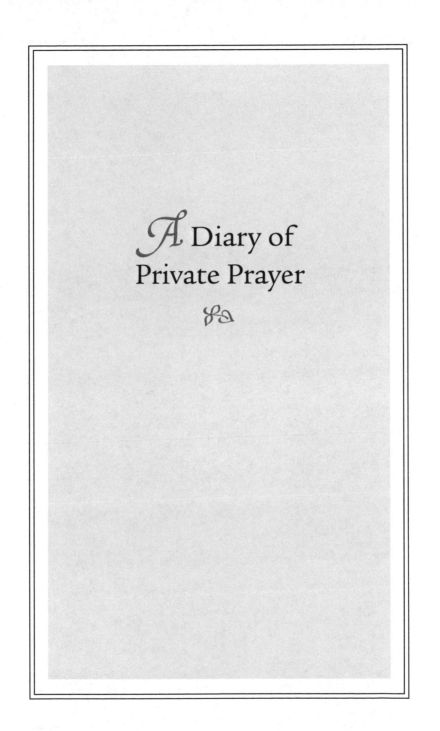

A Diary of
Private Prayer

*E*TERNAL Father of my soul, let my first thought today be of you, let my first impulse be to worship you, let my first word be your Name, let my first action be to kneel before you in prayer.

For your perfect wisdom and perfect goodness;
For the love you have for all people;
For the love you have for me;
For the great and mysterious opportunity of my life;
For your Spirit, who dwells in my heart;
For the seven gifts of your Spirit;
                    I praise and worship you, O Lord.

Yet when this morning prayer is finished, do not let me think that my worship is ended and spend the rest of the day forgetting you. Rather, from these quiet moments, let light and joy and power pour out and remain with me through every hour of this day.

May that light and joy and power:
Keep my thoughts pure;
Keep me gentle and truthful in all I say;
Keep me faithful and diligent in my work;
Keep me humble in my opinion of myself;
Keep me honorable and generous in my dealings with others;
Keep me loyal to every cherished memory of the past;
Keep me mindful of my eternal destiny as your child.

O God, you have been the refuge of your people through many generations; be my refuge in every moment and every need that I face today. Be my guide through all uncertainty and darkness. Be my guard against all that threatens my spiritual well-being. Be my strength in times of testing. Cheer my heart with your peace; through Jesus Christ my Lord. Amen.

O LORD, you are from everlasting to everlasting; I turn my thoughts to you as the hours of darkness and of sleep begin. O Sun of my soul, I rejoice to know that all night I shall be under the watchful eye of the One who dwells in eternal light.

Into your care, Father, I now entrust my body and soul. All day you have watched over me, your companionship has filled my heart with peace. Accompany me throughout the night.

Give me sound and refreshing sleep;
Give me safety from all dangers;
Give me freedom from restless dreams;
Give me control of my thoughts, if I lie awake;
Give me wisdom to remember that the night was made for sleep-
    ing and not for harboring anxious or distressing thoughts.
Give me grace, if I lie awake thinking, to think of you.

My soul is satisfied as with a rich feast,
and my mouth praises you with joyful lips
when I think of you on my bed,
and meditate on you in the watches of the night.

Father, into your hands I commit my family and friends, asking you to keep them safe in soul and body, and to be present in their hearts tonight as a Spirit of power, joy, and rest. I pray for ___ and ___. I pray also for those I work with, those around me, those nearby who are unknown to their neighbors, and all those beyond, whom I don't know but who are dear to you; through Jesus Christ our Lord. Amen.

O GOD my Creator and Redeemer, I cannot go into this day unless you accompany me with your blessing. Do not let the vigor and freshness of the morning, or the glow of health, or the present success of my life deceive me into a false reliance upon my own strength. All these good gifts have come to me from you. They were yours to give and are yours to take away. They are not mine to keep; I am your steward, and only by continuing to depend on you, the Giver, can they be enjoyed with integrity.

Let me then give back into your hands all that you have given me, rededicating to your service all I can do with my mind and body, all my possessions, and all my influence with others. All these are yours to use as you want, Father. All these are yours, Christ Jesus. All these are yours, Holy Spirit. O my Lord, speak in my words today, think in my thoughts, and work in all my actions. Thank you that it is your gracious will to make use of me, even at my weakest, to fulfill your mighty purpose for the world. Let my life today be a channel through which at least a little of your love and compassion may reach the lives of those around me.

In your presence, O God, I remember all my friends and neighbors, those who live in this area, and especially those who are poor, asking you to give me grace to serve them wholeheartedly in your name.

O blessed Jesus, you used your own life for the redemption of your human brothers and sisters. You gave no thought to your comfort or earthly gain, but you filled up your hours and days with deeds of selfless love. Give me grace today to follow the road that you walked; and to your name be all the glory and the praise, even to the end. Amen.

O FATHER in heaven, who crafted my limbs to serve you and my soul to follow closely after you, with sorrow and repentance of heart I acknowledge before you the faults and failures of today. For too long I have tried your patience and too often I have betrayed your trust; yet you still want me to come to you with a humble heart, as I now do, imploring you to drown my sin in the sea of your infinite love.

O Lord, forgive me for:
My failure to be true, even to my own standards;
My excuses in the face of temptation;
My choosing of the worse when I know the better;

O Lord, forgive me for:
My failure to apply to myself the standards I demand of others;
My blindness to the suffering of others, and the time it takes me
    to learn from my own;
My apathy toward wrongs that do not impact me, and my over-
    sensitiveness to those that do.

O Lord, forgive me for:
My slowness to see the good in others and to see the flaws in
    myself;
My hard-heartedness toward the faults of others and my readiness
    to make allowances for my own;
My unwillingness to believe that you have called me to a small
    work and my brother or sister to a great one.

Create in me a clean heart, O God, and put a new and right spirit within me. Do not cast me away from your presence, and do not take your holy spirit from me. Restore to me the joy of your salvation, and sustain in me a willing spirit. Amen.

*L*ORD of my life, whose commands I am eager to keep, whose fellowship I am eager to enjoy, and to whose service I am eager to be loyal, I kneel before you as you send me out to serve you.

Thank you, Lord, for this new day. For its gladness and brightness; for its many hours waiting to be filled with joyful and helpful labor; for its open doors of possibility; for its hope of new beginnings. Stir up in my heart the desire to make the very most of today's opportunities. Do not let me break any of yesterday's promises, or leave unrepaired any of yesterday's wrongs. Do not let me see anyone in distress and pass by on the other side. Give me the strength to confront any mountain of duty or bad habit. Where an action of mine can make this world a better place, where a word of mine can cheer a sad heart or strengthen a weak will, where a prayer of mine can serve Christ's kingdom, there let me act and speak and pray.

This day O Lord—

Give me courtesy;
Give me both gentleness of demeanor and decisiveness of character;
Give me patience;
Give me love;
Give me self-control and faithfulness in my relationships;
Give me sincerity in my speech;
Give me diligence in the work you have given me to do.

O Lord, who when the time was right raised up our Lord and Savior Jesus Christ to enlighten our hearts with the knowledge of your love, grant me the grace to be worthy of his name. Amen.

O LORD, you are most wise, most great, and most holy. In wisdom and power and tender mercy you created me in your own image. You have given me this life, you have given me all I have, and you know where and how I live. You have surrounded me with gracious gifts and situations. You have written your law within my heart.

And in my heart's most secret chamber you are waiting to meet and speak with me, freely offering me your fellowship in spite of all I have done wrong. Help me to take this open road to peace of mind. Help me to approach your presence with humility and reverence, carrying with me the spirit of Jesus. Help me to leave behind all anxieties, all wrong desires, all thoughts of malice toward others, and all hesitancy to surrender my will to yours.

> In your will, O Lord, is my peace.
> You are all my heart desires.
> *Whom have I in heaven but you?*
> *And there is nothing on earth that I desire other than you.*

In your presence, O God, I cannot think only of myself, but also of others:

> Of my friends, especially of ___ and of ___;
> Of those I have worked or played with today;
> Of those who are in sorrow;
> Of those who are bearing the burdens of others;
> Of those who are alone in difficult or remote situations, working
> in lonely outposts of your kingdom.

You are the one God and Father of us all; be near us tonight and graciously watch over us. Hear my prayer for Jesus' sake. Amen.

*A*LMIGHTY and eternal God,
You are hidden from my sight;
You are beyond the understanding of my mind;
Your thoughts are not like my thoughts;
Your ways are past finding out.

Yet you have breathed your Spirit into my spirit;
You have formed my mind to seek you;
You have turned my heart to love you;
You have made me restless for the rest that can be found in you;
You have planted within me a hunger and a thirst that make me
    long for the eternal satisfaction of heaven.

O Lord, I praise your name because you have imprinted a seal on my inner being, not leaving me to my own poor and petty ways, or to be ruled by my passions and desires, but calling me to be an heir to your eternal kingdom! Bless you, Lord, for knocking on my heart's door and reminding me of your presence. Bless you, Lord, for your hand upon my life and for the sure knowledge that however I may falter and fail, your everlasting arms are always underneath me.

O Lord, you alone know what lies before me today; grant that in every hour I may stay close to you. Let me be in the world, but not of it. Let me use this world without abusing it. If I buy, let me be as though I have nothing. If I have nothing, let me be as though I have everything. Do not let me embark on anything today that is not in line with your will for my life, nor shrink from any sacrifice that your will demands. Suggest, direct, and guide every movement of my mind; for my Lord Jesus Christ's sake. Amen.

O Lord, all human hearts lie revealed and open before you. Forbid that I should seek to hide from you anything that I have done or thought or imagined today. All these things that are hidden from others, let me now openly acknowledge in your presence. Let no false shame keep me from confessing the wrongs that proper shame should have kept me from committing.

O Lord, whose tender mercies cover us all, humbly and sorrowfully I crave your forgiveness for the sins of this day:

For every weakening and degrading thought that I have allowed to
   dwell in my mind;
For every hasty and thoughtless word;
For every failure of self-control;
For every stumbling block I have put in someone else's way,
   whether by wrongdoing or bad example;
For every lost opportunity;
For lazy feet and a procrastinating will;
For ___;
And ___;
And ___.

Grant that as the days go by, your Spirit may more and more rule in my heart, giving me victory over these and other sinful ways.

Into your loving care I commit all those who are dear to me, especially ___ and ___. Bless all those with whom I live and work and worship. Grant them a satisfying sense of your reality and power. Be with all those who are in danger or distress tonight. Be in every sore heart, every grief-stricken or broken home, and beside every sickbed giving to all the blessing of your peace. Amen.

G OD of my ancestors, I cry out to you. You have been the refuge of good and wise people in every generation. When history began you were the first to enlighten the minds of men and women, and your Spirit was the first to lead them to realize their full humanity. Throughout the ages you have been the Lord and giver of life, the source of all knowledge, and the fountain of all goodness.

The patriarchs, like Abraham, trusted you and were not put
to shame;
The prophets, like Isaiah, sought you and you put your words
on their lips;
The psalmists, like David, rejoiced in you and you were present
in their songs;
The apostles, like Peter, waited for you and were filled with your
Holy Spirit;
The martyrs, like Stephen, called upon you and you were with
them in the flames;
This poor soul called, and was heard by the Lord, and was saved from
every trouble.

O God, you have always been there, you are with us now, and you endure forever; I thank you for this well-worn Christian path, a road beaten hard by the footsteps of saints, apostles, prophets, and martyrs. Thank you for the signposts and warning signals which are there at every corner and which I can understand through the study of the Bible, and history, and all the great literature of the world. Above all, I give you sincere and humble thanks for the great gift of Jesus Christ, the pioneer of our faith. I praise you that I have been born in an age and a land that have known his name, and that I am not called to face any temptation or trial which he did not first endure.

Holy Lord, help me to profit from these great memories of the ages gone by, and help me to enter into the glorious inheritance which you have prepared for me; through Jesus Christ my Lord. Amen.

*A*LMIGHTY God, in this hour of quiet I seek communion with you. I want to turn away from the worry and fever of today's work, from the world's jarring noises, from the praise and blame of other people, from the confused thoughts and fantasies of my own heart, and instead seek the quietness of your presence. All day long I have been working and striving, but now in stillness of heart and in the clear light of your eternity, I want to think about the pattern my life has been weaving.

May there fall on me now, O God, a great sense of your power and
    your glory, so that I may see all earthly things as they really are.
Help me to know more deeply that with you one day is like a
    thousand years and a thousand years are like one day.
Give me now such a clear understanding of your perfect holiness
    that I may no longer be full of pride in my own achievements.
Give me now such a clear vision of your uncreated beauty that I
    may never be satisfied with anything less.

> *Though earth and man were gone,*
> *And suns and universes cease to be,*
> *And Thou wert left alone,*
> *Every existence would exist in Thee.*

Dear Father, I am content to leave my life in your hands, knowing that you have counted every hair of my head. I am content to give over my will to yours, believing I can find in you a righteousness, an integrity, that I could never have obtained on my own. I am content to leave all my loved ones in your care, believing that your love for them is greater than mine. I am content to leave in your hands the causes of truth and justice and the coming of your kingdom, believing that my passion for them is just a feeble shadow of your steady purpose.

To you, O God, be glory forever. Amen.

O GOD, you have proved your love for all people by sending us Jesus Christ our Lord, and you have illuminated our human life with the radiance of his presence. Thank you for this, your greatest gift. Thank you, God—

For every day my Lord spent on this earth;
For the record of his deeds of love;
For the words he spoke for my guidance and help;
For his obedience, even to death;
For his triumph over death;
For the presence of his Spirit with me now.

Help me, Lord, to remember the blessed life that was once lived out on this common earth, under these ordinary skies. May I take this memory into each task and duty of today.
Help me to remember—

His eagerness to help others, rather than be helped;
His sympathy with suffering of every kind;
His bravery in the face of his own suffering;
His gentleness toward others, so that when he was abused he did not retaliate;
His steadiness of purpose in keeping to his appointed task;
His simplicity;
His self-discipline;
His serenity of spirit;
His complete reliance upon you, his Father in heaven.

In each of these ways give me grace to follow in his footsteps.
Almighty God, Father of our Lord Jesus Christ, I commit all my ways to you. I entrust my soul into your hands. I pledge my life to your service. May this day be for me a day of obedience and love, a day of happiness and peace. May all I do and say be worthy of Christ and his gospel. Amen.

O LORD, you are the only origin of all that is good and fair and true; to you I lift up my soul.

O God, send your Spirit now to enter my heart.
    Now as I pray this prayer, do not let any room within me be secretly closed to keep you out.
O God, give me the power to pursue only what is good.
    Now as I pray this prayer, banish any evil purpose or plan that lurks in my heart waiting for an opportunity to be fulfilled.
O God, bless all my plans and work, and help them to prosper.
    Now as I pray this prayer, do not let me hold on to any plan that I dare not ask you to bless.
O God, give me purity of heart, mind, and body.
    Now as I pray this prayer, do not let me say to myself secretly, *But not yet* or *But not too much.*
O God, bless every member of this household.
    Now as I pray this prayer, do not let me harbor in my heart any jealousy, bitterness, or anger toward any of them.
O God, bless my enemies and all those who have done me wrong.
    Now as I pray this prayer, do not let me cherish in my heart the intention to pay them back as soon as I get an opportunity.
O God, let your Kingdom come on earth.
    Now as I pray this prayer, do not let me still intend in my heart to devote my best hours and years to the service of lesser goals.

O Holy Spirit of God, as I finish this time of prayer, do not let me return to evil thoughts and the ways of the world, but let the same mind be in me that was in Christ Jesus. Amen.

O LORD and Maker of all things, whose creative power made the first ray of light, and who looked on the world's first morning and saw that it was good, I praise you for this light that now streams through my windows to waken me to the life of another day.

I praise you for the life that stirs within me;
I praise you for the bright and beautiful world around me;
I praise you for the earth and sea and sky, for the hurrying clouds
    and singing birds;
I praise you for the work that you have given me to do; for all you
    have given me to fill my hours of leisure;
I praise you for my friends;
I praise you for music and books and good company and all
    harmless and delightful pleasures.

O Lord, you yourself are everlasting Mercy; give me a tender heart today toward all those who in this morning light are less joyful than I am.

Those in whom the pulse of life grows weak;
Those who are unable to get out of bed to enjoy the sunshine;
The blind, who are shut off from the light of day;
The overworked, who have no joy of leisure;
The unemployed, who have no joy of labor;
The bereaved, whose hearts and homes are desolate;
                        Have mercy on them all.

O Light that never fades, as the light of day now streams through these windows and floods this room, so let me open to you the windows of my heart, that all my life may be filled with the radiance of your presence. Do not let any corner of my being be left in darkness, but illuminate every part of me by the light of your face. Do not leave anything within me that could darken the brightness of the day. Let the Spirit of Jesus, whose life was the light of all people, rule within my heart until evening. Amen.

O ETERNAL Being, you live in everlasting light; now as the world's light fades, I seek the brightness of your presence.

You never get weary; now as my limbs grow heavy and my spirit begins to flag, I commit myself to you.

You never sleep; now as I lie down to sleep, I cast myself into your care.

You keep watch eternally; now when I lie helpless, I rely on your love.

Before I sleep, O God, I look back over today in the light of your eternity.

I remember with bitterness the duties I have avoided;
I remember with sorrow the hard words I have spoken;
I remember with shame the unworthy thoughts I have held in my mind.
Use these memories, O God, to save me, and then blot them out forever.
I remember with joy the beauties of the world today;
I remember with sweetness the kindness of others which I have seen today;
I remember with thankfulness the work you have enabled me to do today and the truth you have enabled me to learn.
Use these memories, O God, to humble me, and then let them live forever in my soul.

Before I sleep, let me spend this moment rejoicing in the love and friendships with which you have blessed my life. I rejoice in the dear memory of ___ and ___; knowing that though they have passed into the mystery beyond death, they have not passed beyond your love and care. I rejoice in my continued friendship with ___ and ___; I entrust them, along with myself, into your care through the hours of darkness. O Father, have compassion on all those who have nowhere to sleep, and those who, though lying down, cannot sleep for pain or anxiety. In the name of our Lord Jesus. Amen.

O GOD, who in love and pity sent us Jesus Christ to be the Light in our darkness, give me wisdom to profit from the words he spoke, and grace to follow in his footsteps.

> Jesus said: *Whenever you stand praying, forgive, if you have anything against anyone; so that your Father in heaven may also forgive you your trespasses.*
>> O God, give me the grace to do this now.
> Jesus said: *It is more blessed to give than to receive.*
>> O God, give me grace today not to think of what I can get, but of what I can give.
> Jesus said: *When you give alms, do not let your left hand know what your right hand is doing.*
>> O God, grant that what I give may be given without self-satisfaction and without thought of praise or reward.
> Jesus said: *Enter through the narrow gate.*
>> O God, give me grace today to keep to the narrow path of duty and honest dealing.
> Jesus said: *Do not judge.*
>> O God, give me grace today to take the plank out of my own eye before I look at the speck in my brother's or sister's eye.
> Jesus said: *What good is it for someone to gain the whole world, yet lose their own soul?*
>> O God, give me grace to live this day in such a way that whatever else I lose, I will not lose my soul, my very life in you.

Jesus said: *Then this is how you should pray* [and this, Lord, is how I pray]: *Our Father in heaven, hallowed be your name. Your kingdom come, your will be done, on earth as it is in heaven. Give us today our daily bread. Forgive us our sins, as we forgive those who sin against us. And do not lead us into temptation, but deliver us from evil. For yours is the kingdom, the power, and the glory, for ever and ever. Amen.*

O GOD, the Father of all humankind, I bring before you tonight the burden of the world's life. I join with the scattered multitudes who are crying out to you in their desperation. Hear us, O God, and look with compassion at our many needs, since you alone are able to satisfy all our desire.

I especially commit to you:

All who are far from their family and friends tonight;
All who must lie down hungry or cold;
All who suffer pain;
All who are kept awake by anxiety;
All who are facing danger;
All who must work or keep watch while others sleep.

I ask you to give them all such a sense of your presence that their loneliness may turn to comfort and their trouble to peace.

O most loving God, you showed your love to us in Jesus your Son, by relieving all kinds of suffering and disease. Grant your blessing on all who are serving others in Christ's name throughout the world:

All ministers of the gospel of Christ;
All social workers;
All doctors and nurses who faithfully tend the sick;
All who work for your mission in every land.

Through them accomplish your great purpose of goodwill to all people, and grant them in their own hearts the joy of Christ's very real presence.

Grant to me also, O gracious Father, the joy of a life surrendered to Christ's service and the peace of forgiveness granted through the power of his cross. Amen.

*H*ERE I am, O God, humbly yours, lifting up my heart to you, before whom all created things are as dust and mist. You are hidden behind the curtain of our limited sight and hearing, incomprehensible in your greatness, mysterious in your almighty power; yet here am I, speaking to you with the familiarity of a child to a parent, a friend to a friend. If I could not speak to you like this, then I would indeed be without hope in the world. I have little power to do or control anything; it is not by my will that I am here or will one day pass away. Of all that will come to me today, very little will have been what I have chosen for myself.

It is you, O hidden One, who has given me my heritage, and you determined the place of my birth. It is you who have given me the power to do one kind of work and have withheld the skill to do another. It is you who hold in your hand the threads of this day's life and you alone who know what lies before me to do or to suffer. But because you are my Father, I am not afraid. Because it is your Spirit that stirs within my heart's most secret room, I know that all is well. What I desire for myself I cannot achieve; but whatever you desire in me you can help me to achieve. The good that I want to do, I fail to do, but you can give me the power to do good.

Dear Father, take this day's life into your keeping. Guide all my thoughts and feelings. Direct all my energies. Instruct my mind. Sustain my will. Take my hands and give me the skill to serve you. Take my feet and make them quick to do whatever you ask. Take my eyes and keep them fixed on your everlasting beauty. Take my mouth and give me the words to tell others of your love. Make this day a day of obedience, a day of spiritual joy and peace. Make this day's work a little part of the work of the kingdom of my Lord Jesus, in whose name these prayers are said. Amen.

O MERCIFUL Father, you look on the weaknesses of your human children more in pity than in anger, and more in love than in pity. Help me now in your holy presence to examine the secrets of my heart.

Have I done anything today to fulfill the purpose for which you
  brought me into the world?
Have I accepted the opportunities of service that in your wisdom
  you have put before me?
Have I performed the duties of the day without leaving any undone?
        Give me grace to answer honestly, Lord.

Have I done anything today to damage the Christian ideal of true
  humanity?
Have I been lazy in body or listless in spirit?
Have I overindulged my bodily appetites?
Have I kept my imagination pure and healthy?
Have I been scrupulously honorable in all my dealings?
Have I been transparently sincere in all I have claimed to be, to feel,
  or to do?
        Give me grace to answer honestly, Lord.

Have I tried today to see myself as others see me?
Have I made more excuses for myself than I have been willing to
  make for others?
Have I been a peacemaker in my own home, or have I stirred up
  trouble?
Have I, while professing noble convictions for great causes, failed
  even in common charity and courtesy toward those nearest to me?
        Give me grace to answer honestly, Lord.

Lord, it is only your infinite love, demonstrated to us in Jesus Christ, which has the power to destroy the empire of evil in my heart. Grant that with each day that passes I may more and more be delivered from the sins that keep tempting me. Amen.

O GOD, *you are my God; I seek you, my soul thirsts for you; my flesh faints for you, as in a dry and weary land where there is no water. So I have looked upon you in the sanctuary, beholding your power and glory. Because your steadfast love is better than life, my lips will praise you.*

Seven times a day I praise you for your righteous ordinances. Great peace have those who love your law; nothing can make them stumble.

How can young people keep their way pure? By guarding it according to your word.

Make me to know your ways, O Lord; teach me your paths. Lead me in your truth, and teach me, for you are the God of my salvation; for you I wait all day long.

Set a guard over my mouth, O Lord; keep watch over the door of my lips.

Keep my steps steady according to your promise, and never let iniquity have dominion over me.

O Lord, who may abide in your tent? Who may dwell on your holy hill? Those who walk blamelessly, and do what is right, and speak the truth from their heart; who do not slander with their tongue, and do no evil to their friends, nor take up a reproach against their neighbors; in whose eyes the wicked are despised, but who honor those who fear the Lord; who stand by their oath even to their hurt; who do not lend money at interest, and do not take a bribe against the innocent. Those who do these things shall never be moved.

Let the words of my mouth and the meditation of my heart be acceptable to you, O Lord, my rock and my redeemer. Amen.

*A*LMIGHTY God, thank you for your love which follows me every day of my life. Thank you that you fill my mind with your divine truth and strengthen my will with your divine grace. Thank you for every indication of your Spirit leading me, and for the things that seem like chance or coincidence at the time, but later appear to me as part of your gracious plan for my spiritual growth. Help me to follow where you lead and never quench this light that you have ignited within me, rather let me grow daily in grace and in the knowledge of Jesus my Lord.

Yet as I seek your presence I do not want to pray only for myself. I bring before you all my human brothers and sisters who need your help. Especially tonight I think of—

> those who are faced with great temptations;
> those who are faced with tasks too difficult for them;
> those who stand in any valley of decision;
> those who are in debt or poverty;
> those who are suffering the consequences of actions which they repented of long ago;
> those who through no fault of their own have had little chance in life;
> all family circles broken by death;
> all missionaries of the kingdom of heaven in every corner of the earth;
> those who lift high the lamp of truth in lonely places;
> and ___ and ___ and ___.

Dear Father of all, make me a human channel through which, as far as I am able, your divine love and pity may reach the hearts and lives of some of those who are nearest to me. Amen.

*L*ORD, you are everywhere, and it is beneath your eye that all lives are lived; please grant that all my purposes and actions today may be honorable and gracious. May I be just and true in all my dealings. May no mean or unworthy thought have a moment's place in my mind. May my motives be transparent to all. May my word be my bond. May I not take unfair advantage of anyone. May I be kind in my judgment of others. May I be unbiased in my opinions. May I be loyal to my friends and generous to my opponents. May I face adversity with courage. May I not ask or expect too much for myself.

Yet, Lord, do not let me rest content with an ideal of humanity that is less than what was shown to us in Jesus. Give me the mind of Christ. May I not rest until I am like him in all his fullness. May I listen to Jesus' question: *What are you doing more than others?* And so may the three Christian graces of faith, hope, and love be more and more formed within me, until all I do and say brings honor to Jesus and his gospel.

O God, you proved your love to us in the passion and death of Jesus Christ our Lord; may the power of his cross be with me today. May I love as he loved. May I be obedient even to death. As I lean on his cross may I not refuse my own; but rather may I bear it by the strength of his.

O Lord, you have placed the solitary in families; I ask for your heavenly blessing for all the members of my household, all my neighbors, and all my fellow citizens. May Christ rule in every heart and his law be honored in every home. May every knee bend before him and every tongue confess that he is Lord. Amen.

O MERCIFUL heart of God, in true penitence and remorse I open my heart to you now. Let me keep nothing hidden from you while I pray. The truth about myself is humbling, but give me courage to speak it out in your presence. What I was not too ashamed to commit, may I not be too ashamed to confess. In your wisdom use this pain of confession as a way of making me hate the sins confessed.

I confess to laziness in this ___ and this ___;
I confess to vanity in this ___ and this ___;
I confess to this ___ and this ___ indulgence in physical desires;
I confess to the habit of lying in this ___ and this ___;
I confess to this ___ and this ___ dishonesty;
I confess to this ___ and this ___ unkind word;
I confess to having entertained this ___ and this ___ evil thought;
I confess to this ___ and this ___ wrong direction my life has been taking;
I confess to this ___ and this ___ lapse from faithful Christian living.

O Lord, whose love in the human heart can burn like a fire all that is shameful and evil, let me now grasp your perfect righteousness and make it my own. Blot out all my disobedience and let my sins be covered. Help me to feel your hand upon my life, cleansing me from the stain of past wrongdoings, loosing me from the grip of evil habits, strengthening me in new habits of pure heartedness and guiding my footsteps in the way of eternal life. O God, lead me in battle against my secret sins. Fence around my life with a shield of hope and commitment. And let Christ be formed in my heart through faith. All this I ask for his holy name's sake. Amen.

O ETERNAL God, although I cannot see you with my eyes or touch you with my hands, give me today a clear conviction of your reality and power. Do not let me go into my work believing only in the world of sense and time, but give me grace to understand that the world I cannot see or touch is the most real world of all. My life today will be lived in time, but it will involve eternal issues. The needs of my body will shout out, but it is for the needs of my soul that I must care the most. My business will be with material things, but let me be aware of spiritual things behind them. Let me always keep in mind that the things that matter are not money or possessions, not houses or property, not bodily comforts or pleasures, but truth and honor and gentleness and helpfulness and a pure love of you.

Thank you, Lord:

For the power you have given me to grasp things unseen;
For the strong sense I have that this is not my eternal home;
For my restless heart which nothing finite can satisfy.

Thank you, Lord:

For sending your Spirit to fill my heart;
For all human love and goodness that speak to me of you;
For the fullness of your glory poured out in Jesus Christ.

On my pilgrim journey toward eternity, I come before you, the eternal One. Let me not try to deaden or destroy the desire for you that disturbs my heart. Let me rather give myself over to its persuasion and go where it leads me. Make me wise today to see all things within the dimension of eternity and make me brave to face all the changes in my life that come from this vision; through the grace of Christ my Savior. Amen.

O LORD, all treasures of wisdom and truth and holiness are stored up in your boundless being. Grant that through our constant fellowship with you, those graces of Christian character may more and more take shape within me:

The grace of a thankful and uncomplaining heart;
The grace to await your timing patiently and to answer your call promptly;
The grace of courage whether in suffering or in danger;
The grace to endure any hardship in the fight against evil;
The grace of boldness to stand up for what is right;
The grace of being adequately prepared for any temptation;
The grace of physical discipline;
The grace of truthfulness;
The grace to treat others as I would like them to treat me;
The grace of sensitivity, that I may refrain from hasty judgment;
The grace of silence, that I may refrain from thoughtless speech;
The grace of forgiveness toward all who have wronged me;
The grace of tenderness toward all who are weaker than myself;
The grace of faithfulness in continuing to desire that you will answer these prayers.

And now, O God, give me a quiet mind as I lie down to rest. Dwell in my thoughts until sleep overtakes me. Do not let me be worried by the small anxieties of this life. Do not let any troubled dreams disturb me, so that I may wake refreshed and ready for all that tomorrow brings.

And Thou, O Lord, by whom are seen
Thy creatures as they be,
Forgive me if too close I lean
My human heart on Thee. Amen.

O LORD, you are the hidden Source of all life. Help me now to meditate on your great and gracious plan that a mere mortal like me should look up to you and call you Father.

In the beginning you, the uncreated, released your creative power;
And then space and time and matter;
The atom and the molecule and crystalline forms;
The first germ of life;
And then the long upward striving of life;
The things that creep and fly, the animals of the forest, the birds of the air, the fish of the sea;
And then the gradual dawn of intelligence;
And at last the making of human beings;
The beginning of history;
The first altar and the first prayer.

O hidden love of God, it is your will that all created spirits should live forever in pure and perfect fellowship with you. Grant that in my life today I may do nothing to defeat this, your most gracious purpose. Help me to keep in mind that your whole creation is groaning in labor pains as we wait for the revealing of the children of God; and let me welcome every influence of your Spirit upon my spirit that may make this happen more speedily.

When you knock on the door of my heart, may I never keep you standing outside, but welcome you in with joy and thanksgiving. May I never harbor anything in my heart that I would be ashamed of in your presence; may I never keep a single corner closed to your influence.

Do what you will with me, O God; make of me what you will, change me as you will, and use me as you will, both now and in the larger life beyond; through Jesus Christ our Lord. Amen.

O HEAVENLY Father, give me a heart like the heart of Jesus, a heart more ready to serve than be served, a heart moved by compassion towards the weak and oppressed, a heart set upon the coming of your kingdom in the world of men and women.

I pray tonight, O God, for all the different kinds of people to whom Jesus gave special concern and care when he was on earth:

For those needing food or drink or clothes;
For the sick and all those who are wasted by disease;
For the blind;
For the disabled;
For people suffering from life-shattering diseases like leprosy in
    Jesus' time and HIV/AIDS in ours;
For prisoners;
For those oppressed by any injustice, and for refugees and asylum
    seekers;
For the homeless, and all the lost sheep of our society;
For all victims of sexual exploitation and abuse;
For the lonely;
For all single parents;
For the worried and the anxious;
For those who are living faithful lives in obscurity;
For those who are fighting bravely for unpopular causes;
For all those who are working diligently for you throughout your
    world.

Grant, O Father, that your loving kindness in giving me so much may not make me less sensitive to the needs of others less fortunate, but rather move me to lay their burdens on my own heart. If I should experience any adversity, help me not to brood on my own sorrows, as if I were alone in the world of suffering; but rather help me to take time to serve, with compassion, those who need my help. Let the power of my Lord Jesus Christ be strong within me and his peace invade my spirit. Amen.

O LORD, you indwell our shabby human life, lifting it now and then above the dominance of animal passion and greed, allowing it to shine with borrowed lights of love and joy and peace, and making it a mirror of the beauties of a world unseen. Grant that my part in the world's life today may not be to obscure the splendor of your presence but rather to make it more plainly visible to the eyes of my fellow men and women.

Help me to make a stand today—

for whatever is pure, true, just, and good;
for the advancement of science and education and true learning;
for the redemption of daily business from the blight of self-seeking;
for the rights of the weak and the oppressed;
for cooperation and mutual help in industry, commerce, and
    government;
for the conservation of the rich traditions of the past;
for the recognition of new movements of your Spirit in the minds
    and lives of people today;
for the hope of even more glorious days to come.

Today, dear Lord—

Help me put what is right before my own interest;
Help me put others before myself;
Help me not to forget matters of the spirit, by being too consumed
    with matters of the body;
Help me put the attainment of what is true and just and honor-
    able above the enjoyment of present pleasures;
Help me put principle above reputation;
Help me put you above all else.

O God, the reflection of your transcendent glory once appeared unbroken in the face of Jesus Christ. Give me today a heart like his: a brave heart, a true heart, a tender heart, a heart with great room in it, a heart fixed on you; for his name's sake. Amen.

O DIVINE Love, as you stand outside the closed doors of human hearts and knock, grant me the grace to throw open all the doors of my heart. Tonight let me draw back every bolt and bar that until now has robbed my life of air and light and love.

Open my ears, O God, so that I can hear your voice calling me to attempt great things. Too often when you have spoken to me I have been deaf to your appeals; but now give me the courage to answer, *Here I am; send me.* Help me to hear when any of my human brothers and sisters, your children, call out in need. Help me to hear your voice in their cry.

Open my mind, O God, so that I may welcome any new insights or knowledge that you wish to give me. May I not cling to the past so tightly that I limit the life ahead of me. Give me courage to change my mind when that is needed. Help me to be tolerant to the thoughts of others and open to the truths they may teach me.

Open my eyes, O God, so that I may see you in your wonderful creation around me. Let all lovely things fill my heart with joy, and may they turn my mind to your everlasting loveliness. Forgive me for the times when I have been blind to the grandeur and glory of creation, the charm of little children, and the beauty of human lives, and so have failed to see you in all these reminders of your presence.

Open my hands, O God: hands ready to share with others all the blessings you have so richly given me. Deliver me from all mean and selfish instincts. All my money is yours and all my possessions belong to you; help me to be a faithful steward of your generosity. All honor and glory be to you forever. Amen.

O GOD, you are alive from eternity to eternity. You are not just at one time or in one place, because all times and places are in you. I long to understand my destiny as a child of yours. Here I stand, weak and mortal amid the immensities of nature. But blessed are you, O Lord God, for you have made me in your own likeness, and you have breathed into me the breath of your own life. Within this fragile body you have set a spirit that can relate to your own Spirit. Within this perishable being you have planted what cannot perish, and within this mortal, immortality. So from this little room and this early hour I can lift up my mind beyond all time and space to you, the uncreated One, until the light of your face illuminates my whole life.

Let me remember that my mortal body is only the servant of my immortal soul;

Let me remember how uncertain my hold is on my own physical life;

Let me remember that here I have no continuing city, but only a place for a brief stay, and a time for testing and training;

Let me use this world without abusing it;

Let me be in this world but not of it;

Let me be as though I have nothing, and yet possess everything;

Let me understand the vanity of what is time bound and the glory of the eternal;

Let my world be centered not in myself, but in you.

Almighty God, you raised your Son from the dead and set him at your right hand in everlasting glory. Thank you for this hope of immortality with which, through many ages, you have cheered and enlightened the souls of your people; a hope which you have made secure through our Lord Jesus Christ. Amen.

O GOD of mercy, you care for me as if you had no other to care for, and yet you care for all others as you care for me; so I bring to you my needs and also the needs of the world of humankind to which I belong.

Remember me in your mercy, O God, and keep me in your grace. Forgive the poor use I have made today of the talents you have entrusted to me. Cover up the inadequacy of my service by the fullness of your resources. Yet grant also that day by day I may be strengthened by your help, so that my service may grow less unworthy and my sins less grievous. May Christ more and more reign in my heart and purify my deeds.

Remember in your mercy all humankind, O God. Let the whole earth be filled with your praise and made glad by the knowledge of your name. Let there fall upon all people a sense of your excellent greatness. Let the nations be in awe of you. Let your glory rule over every seat of power and every workplace. Let your law be honored in every home. Redeem the whole world's life, O God, and transform it utterly through the power of the cross.

O Lord, you graciously use our small human efforts toward the attainment of your purposes. I pray for all who are devoting their lives to proclaiming the gospel in every land, especially ___ and ___. I pray for all who are working for the cause of peace and understanding between nations, and for all who are striving to break down the dividing walls between enemies and to make all one in Christ Jesus. Encourage them with the joy of your presence, and kindle in me the urgent desire to further and support their hard work as far as I am able; through Jesus Christ. Amen.

*M*Y SOUL *yearns for you in the night; my spirit within me earnestly seeks you. For when your judgments are in the earth, the inhabitants of the world learn righteousness.*

O God, give me today a strong and vivid sense that you are by my side. In a crowd or by myself, in business and leisure, in my sitting down and my rising, may I always be aware of your presence beside me. By your grace, O God, I will go nowhere today where you cannot come, nor seek anyone's presence that would rob me of yours. By your grace I will let no thought enter my heart that might hinder my closeness with you, nor let any word come from my mouth that is not meant for your ear. So shall my courage be firm and my heart be at peace.

> *I steadier step*
> *When I recall*
> *That though I slip*
> *Thou dost not fall.*

O Lord, the desired of all nations, in the knowledge of your love and power there is salvation for all the peoples of the earth. Quickly bring the day when everyone shall acknowledge you as Lord over all. Quickly bring the day when our earthly society shall become the kingdom of Christ. Quickly bring the day when your presence and the strong hand of your purpose shall be found not only in the hearts of a few wise and brave people, but throughout the nation, in the corridors of power, in the workshop, office, and marketplace, in the city and in the country. And whatever I myself can do toward the fulfilment of your purpose, give me grace to begin today, through Jesus Christ. Amen.

O LORD, your eternal love for all people was most perfectly shown in the blessed life and death of our Lord Jesus. Enable me now to meditate so deeply on my Lord's passion, that as I have fellowship with him in his sorrow, I may learn the secret of his strength and peace.

I remember Gethsemane;
I remember how Judas betrayed him;
I remember how Peter denied him;
I remember how *all of them deserted him and fled*;
I remember the scourging;
I remember the crown of thorns;
I remember how they spat on him;
I remember how they struck him on the head with a staff;
I remember his pierced hands and feet;
I remember his agony on the cross;
I remember his thirst;
I remember how he cried, *"My God, My God, why have you forsaken me?"*

> *We may not know, we cannot tell,*
> *What pains He had to bear;*
> *But we believe it was for us*
> *He hung and suffered there.*

Grant, O most gracious God, that as I kneel before you I may be embraced in the great company of those whom you have saved and brought to life through the cross of Christ. Let the redeeming power that has flowed from his sufferings through so many generations now flow into my soul. Here let me find forgiveness of sin. Here let me learn to share with Christ the burden of the suffering world. Amen.

*A*LMIGHTY God, you are always present in the world around me, in my spirit within me, and in the unseen world beyond me; let me carry with me through this day's life a most real sense of your power and glory.

O God around me, forbid that I should look at the work of your hands today and give no thought to you, the Maker. Let the heavens declare your glory to me and the hills speak of your majesty. Let every fleeting loveliness I see speak to me of a loveliness that does not fade. Let the beauty of the earth be to me a sacrament which makes real the beauty of holiness revealed in Jesus Christ my Lord.

O God within me, give me grace today to recognize the stirrings of your Spirit within my soul and to listen most attentively to all that you have to say to me. Do not let the noises of this world so confuse me that I cannot hear you speak. Help me never to deceive myself about the meaning of your commands; and so help me in all things to obey your will, through the grace of Jesus Christ my Lord.

O God beyond me, you dwell in unapproachable light. Teach me that even my highest thoughts of you are but a dim and distant shadow of your transcendent glory. Teach me that if you are in nature, you are still greater than nature. Teach me that if you are in my heart, you are still greater than my heart. Let my soul rejoice in your mysterious greatness. Let me take refuge in the thought that you are utterly beyond me, beyond the sweep of my imagination, beyond the comprehension of my mind. Your judgments are unsearchable and your ways past finding out.

O Lord, hallowed be your name. Amen.

1 BLESS you, most holy God, for your unfathomable love. Through that love you enable Spirit to meet with spirit, so that I, a weak and wandering mortal, can have ready access to your heart, the heart of the One who moves the stars.

With bitterness and anguish of heart, I acknowledge before you the ugly and selfish thoughts that I so often allow to enter my mind and to influence my actions.

I confess, O God—

that often I let my mind wander down unworthy and forbidden ways;

that often I deceive myself as to where my first duty lies;

that often, by concealing my real motives, I pretend to be better than I am;

that often my honesty is only a matter of policy;

that often my affection for my friends is only a refined way of caring for myself;

that often my sparing of my adversary is due to nothing more than cowardice;

that often I do good deeds only so they may be seen by others, and avoid evil ones only because I fear they may be found out.

O holy One, let the fire of your love enter my heart and burn up this tangled mass of meanness and hypocrisy and make my heart like the heart of a little child.

Give me grace, O God, to pray now, with a pure and sincere desire, for all those I have met today. Let me now remember my friends with love and my adversaries with forgiveness, entrusting them all, as I now entrust my own soul and body, to your protecting care; through Jesus Christ. Amen.

O LORD, your eternal presence is hidden behind the veil of nature, enlightens the mind of all people, and was made flesh in Jesus Christ our Lord. I thank you that he has left me an example to follow in his steps.

Jesus said, *Do not store up for yourselves treasures on earth . . . but store up for yourselves treasures in heaven.*
O God, move my heart to follow in this way.
Jesus said, *Strive first for the kingdom of God and his righteousness.*
O God, move my heart to follow in this way.
Jesus said, *Do good . . . and lend . . . expecting to get nothing in return.*
O God, move my heart to follow in this way.
Jesus said, *Love your enemies.*
O God, move my heart to follow in this way.
Jesus said, *Do not fear. Only believe . . .*
O God, move my heart to follow in this way.
Jesus said, *Unless you change and become like children, you will never enter the kingdom of heaven.*
O God, move my heart to follow in this way.
Jesus said, *Ask, and it will be given to you; search, and you will find; knock, and the door will be opened for you.*
O God, move my heart to follow in this way.

Our Father in heaven, hallowed be your name, your kingdom come, your will be done on earth as it is in heaven. Give us today our daily bread. And forgive us our sins, as we forgive those who sin against us. And do not lead us into temptation, but deliver us from evil. For the kingdom, the power, and the glory are yours now and forever. Amen.

O DIVINE Father, your mercy is always waiting for those who return to you in true humility and repentance of heart. So I ask you now to hear this humble seeker who needs your help. How confidently I set out this morning into the life of a new day; now I lie down ashamed and burdened with memories of things undone that ought to have been done and things done that ought not to have been done. Bring me afresh, O God, your healing and cleansing power, so that again I may take hold of the salvation which you have offered to me through Jesus Christ my Lord.

Have mercy upon me, O God—

for my deceitful heart and crooked thoughts;
for harsh words spoken deliberately;
for thoughtless words spoken hastily;
for envious and prying eyes;
for ears that rejoice in what is wrong, and do not rejoice in the
    truth;
for greedy hands;
for feet that have been lazy and gone into the wrong places;
for proud and disdainful looks.

If we say that we have no sin, we deceive ourselves, and the truth is not in us.

Almighty God, Spirit of purity and grace, in asking your forgiveness I cannot claim a right to be forgiven but can only cast myself on your boundless love.

I can plead no merit of my own;
I can plead no extenuating circumstance;
I cannot plead the frailty of my nature;
I cannot plead the force of the temptations I encounter;
I cannot plead the pressure of others who led me astray;
I can only say, for the sake of Jesus Christ, your Son, my Lord.
    Amen.

I BLESS you, most gracious God, that again you have brought light out of darkness and caused the morning to appear! I bless you, because you send me out, in health and life, to the duties and activities of another day! Lord, I ask you to go with me through all the sunlit hours and protect me from every evil way, so that when evening comes, I do not need to hide my head in shame.

Lord, in your gracious love you have called me to be your servant, and I hold myself in readiness today for even your smallest command. Give me the spirit to keep myself in continual training for the prompt fulfillment of your most holy will.

Help me keep the edges of my mind keen;
Help me keep my thinking straight and true;
Help me keep my passions in control;
Help me keep my will active;
Help me keep my body fit and healthy;
Help me remember him whose food it was to do the will of the
    One who sent him.

O Lord of every workplace, bless all who truly desire to serve you by being diligent and faithful in their many callings, bearing their share of the world's burden and going about their daily tasks with simplicity and uprightness of heart.

Dear Lord, I pray—

for all who work on the land and with nature;
for all whose work involves sheer physical labor in factories, building sites, mines, and transport;
for all who buy and sell in the marketplace;
for all who labor with their mind;
for all who labor with their pens and computers;
for all whose work is the caring ministry of home and family.

In your great mercy, save us all from the temptations that constantly surround us, and bring us to everlasting life, by the power of the cross. Amen.

*M*ost gracious God, I rejoice in the love you have shown to our poor human race, opening up to us a path of deliverance from our sin and foolishness.

O God the Father, I praise you for your great and holy love. When we had utterly gone astray, you diligently sought us out and saved us, sending your beloved Son to suffer and die so that we might be restored into fellowship with you.

O God the Son, I praise you for your great and holy love. You humbled yourself for the sake of me and all people; you shared in our common life; you dwelt in the midst of all our sin and shame. You endured all the bitterness of the passion and died at last on the cross, so that we might be released from the shackles of sin and enter with you into the glorious freedom of the children of God.

O God the Holy Spirit, I praise you for your great and holy love. You daily pour into my heart the peace and joy of sin forgiven, so that I may share with all the saints in the blessings of my Lord's incarnation, of his passion and crucifixion, and of his resurrection and ascension to the Father's right hand.

O holy and blessed Trinity, help me to dwell so fully in the mystery of this heavenly love that all hatred and malice may be rooted out from my heart and life. Help me to love you, as you first loved me; and in loving you help me also to love my neighbor; and in loving you and my neighbor help me to be saved from all false love of myself; and to you, Father, Son, and Holy Spirit, be all glory and praise forever. Amen.

*A*LMIGHTY God, in your infinite wisdom you have set my life within the narrow bounds of time and circumstance; so let me now go out into the world with a brave and trusting heart. It has pleased you to hold back from me a knowledge of everything; therefore give me the grace of faith so that I may grasp what I cannot see. You have given me little power to shape things to my own desires; therefore use your own great power to make what you desire happen within me. It is your will that through hard work and suffering I should walk the upward road; so be my fellow traveler as I go.

Let me face what you send with the strength you supply;
When you make what I do effective, help me to ensure that your word is effective in my heart;
When you call me to go through the dark valley, do not let me persuade myself that I know a way around;
Help me not to refuse any opportunity to help other people that may come today, nor fall into any temptation that may lie in wait for me;
Do not let the sins of yesterday be repeated in the life of today, or the life of today set any evil example to the life of tomorrow.

O God of my ancestors, in every age you have enlightened the souls of the faithful. Thank you for the gift of shared memories through which the great stories of the past live with us today. Thank you for the lives of the saints, and for the help I can gain from their example. Thank you for the memory of ___ and ___; for the apostles, prophets, and martyrs; but most of all for the incarnation of your dear Son, in whose name these prayers are said. Amen.

I CALL *upon you, O Lord: come quickly to me; give ear to my voice when I call to you. Let my prayer be counted as incense before you, and the lifting up of my hands as an evening sacrifice.*

O Lord, open my lips, and my mouth will declare your praise.

Bless the Lord, O my soul, and do not forget all his benefits:
who forgives all your iniquity;
who heals all your diseases;
who redeems your life from the pit;
who crowns you with steadfast love and mercy;
who satisfies you with good as long as you live so that your youth is renewed like the eagle's.

But who can detect their errors? Clear me from hidden faults. Keep back your servant also from the insolent; do not let them have dominion over me. Then I shall be blameless, and innocent of great transgression.

Have mercy on me, O God, according to your steadfast love; according to your abundant mercy blot out my transgressions. Wash me thoroughly from my iniquity, and cleanse me from my sin. For I know my transgressions, and my sin is ever before me.

Be to me a rock of refuge, a strong fortress, to save me, for you are my rock and my fortress.

I will both lie down and sleep in peace; for you alone, O Lord, make me lie down in safety. Amen.

O HOLY Spirit, visit my soul and stay within me all day. Inspire all my thoughts. Pervade all my imaginations. Suggest all my decisions. Make your home in the most secret place of my will and inspire all my actions. Be with me in my silence and in my speech, in my hurry and in my leisure, in company and in solitude, in the freshness of the morning and in the weariness of the evening; and give me grace at all times to rejoice in the comforting mystery of your companionship.

My heart an altar, and Thy love the flame.

O Spirit unseen, be with me today wherever I go, but also stay with me when I am at home and among my family. Do not let me fail to show those nearest me the sympathy and consideration that you graciously help me to show other people. Do not let me refuse to show those closest to me the courtesy and kindness which I would show to strangers. Let charity begin at home today.

Do not leave me, gracious Presence, while I am absorbing information, through reading books or through the media—newspapers, radio, television, film, and the Internet. Guide me to choose the right books, papers, and programs, and, having chosen them, to use the information they offer in the right way. When I study, grant that all the knowledge I gain may lead me nearer to you. When I read, watch, or listen for recreation, grant that what I read, see, and hear may not lead me away from you. Let all the knowledge I absorb refresh my mind in a way that makes me more eagerly seek whatever is pure and fair and true.

Give me a special sense of your nearness to me, O God, in all the times I devote to private prayer, to sharing in public worship, or to receiving the blessed sacrament; through Jesus Christ my Lord. Amen.

O CREATOR of all things, I lift up my heart in gratitude to you for the happiness I have found today:

For the sheer joy of living;
For all the sights and sounds around me;
For the sweet peace of the country and the bustle of the town;
For friendship and good company;
For work to do and the skill and strength to do it;
For a time to rest and play and for health and a glad heart
    to enjoy it.

Yet let me never think, O eternal Father, that I am here to stay. Let me always remember that I am a stranger and pilgrim on earth. *For here we have no lasting city, but we are looking for the city that is to come.* Lord, by your grace prevent me from losing myself so much in the joys of earth that I have no longing left for the purer joys of heaven. Do not let the happiness of today become a trap to my overworldly heart. And if today instead of happiness I have suffered any disappointment or defeat, if there has been any sorrow where I hoped for joy, or sickness where I looked for health, give me grace to accept it as a loving reminder that this is not my home.

Thank you, Lord, that you have set eternity so firmly in my heart that no earthly thing can ever fully satisfy me. Thank you that every present joy is so mixed with sadness and unrest that it makes my mind look up to the prospect of a more perfect joy. Above all, thank you for the sure hope and promise of eternal life in your presence, which you have given me in the glorious gospel of Jesus Christ my Lord. Amen.

O LORD my God, I kneel before you in humble adoration as I set out to face the tasks and interests of another day. Thank you for the blessed assurance that I shall not be called upon to face them alone or in my own strength, but that at all times I will be accompanied by your presence and strengthened by your grace. Thank you that throughout our human life run the footprints of our Lord and Savior Jesus Christ, who for our sake was made flesh and tasted all the different challenges of humanity. Thank you that as I go about my work today, I can be conscious of the spiritual presence of the heavenly host. Thank you for the saints who rest from their labors, the patriarchs, prophets, and apostles, for the noble martyrs, for all holy and humble people, for my own dear departed friends, especially ___. As I remember them I bless and adore your great name. I rejoice, O God, that you have called me to be a member of the Church of Christ. Let the awareness of this holy fellowship follow me wherever I go, cheering me in loneliness, protecting me in company, strengthening me against temptation, and encouraging me to act in love and justice.

O Lord Jesus Christ, you called the disciples to shine as lights in a dark world. In shame and repentance of heart I acknowledge before you the many faults and weaknesses of which we are guilty, we who in this generation represent your Church to the world. I especially acknowledge my own part in this. Forgive me, I pray, the feebleness of my own witness, the meagerness of my giving and my loving, and the mediocrity of my zeal. Make me a more worthy follower of the One who cared for the poor and the oppressed. Let your power, O Christ, be in us all, to share the world's suffering and redress its wrongs. Amen.

*N*ow, O Lord, when the day's work is done, I turn once more to you. All comes from you, all lives in you, all ends in you. In the morning I set out with your blessing, all day you have upheld me by your grace, and now I pray that you will grant me rest and peace. I cast all my cares upon you and leave to you the outcome of all my work. I pray that you will prosper all that has been done today in accordance with your will, and forgive all that has been done wrong. What good I have done today, graciously accept and use; and if I have done any harm, annul and overrule it by your almighty power.

O Lord, I remember before you tonight all the workers of the world:

Those whose work is mainly physical and those whose work is
     mainly intellectual;
Those working in the cities or on the land;
Those who go out to work and those who keep the home;
Employers and employees;
Those who give orders and those who obey;
Those whose work is dangerous;
Those whose work is monotonous or demeaning;
Those who work against their will for little or no pay;
Those who can find no work to do;
Those whose work is the service of the poor or the healing of the
     sick or the proclamation of the gospel of Christ at home or
     overseas.

Lord Jesus, who came not to be served but to serve, have mercy on all who work faithfully to serve the common good. Lord Jesus, who fed hungry crowds with loaves and fishes, have mercy on all those who have to endure physical hardship to earn their bread for a single day. Lord Jesus, who called all those who are weary and carrying heavy burdens to come to you, have mercy upon all those whose work is beyond their strength. And to you, with the Father and the Holy Spirit, be all the glory and praise. Amen.

*H*OLY Father, from whom all good things come, let the Christian gifts of faith, hope, and love be more firmly established in me every day.

O God, I believe—

that you rule all things in wisdom and righteousness;
that you have called me to be your loyal servant;
that you have the right to call me to complete obedience to your will;
that in Jesus Christ you have shown me a way of salvation, so that I may be delivered from my sins;
that if I truly repent, you are willing to forgive and save me.

O God, I hope—

for your daily mercies to continue;
for the loosening of sin's grip upon my will;
for my growth in grace and in true holiness from day to day;
for a more perfect holiness, when my earthly days are finished;
for a day when I shall know fully, even as I am fully known.

O God, I love you—

who yourself are love;
who in love created me, and in love still cherish me;
who loved me so much that you sent your Son to suffer and die so that I might live with you;
who have commanded me to show my love to you by loving my neighbor for your sake.

Help me in my unbelief, O God; give me greater patience in my hope; and make me more faithful in my love. In loving let me believe and in believing let me love; and in loving and in believing let me hope for a more perfect love and a more unwavering faith; through Jesus Christ my Lord. Amen.

O EVERLASTING God, let the light of your eternity fall now upon my passing days. O holy God, let the light of your perfect righteousness fall upon my sinful ways. O most compassionate God, let the light of your love pierce to the most secret corners of my heart and overcome the darkness of sin within me.

Am I living as my conscience approves?

Am I demanding of others a higher standard of behavior than I demand of myself?

Am I less charitable about the failings of my neighbors than I am about my own?

Am I standing in public for principles which I do not practice in private?

  Let my answer before you be truthful, O God.

Do I ever allow physical satisfaction to take precedence over spiritual interests?

Which is my priority when my course is not clear?

Do I ever allow my own interests to take precedence over the interests of the community?

Which is my priority when my course is not clear?

  Let my answer before you be truthful, O God.

Am I, in my daily life, facing the stress of circumstances with strength and courage?

Am I grateful for my many blessings?

Am I allowing my happiness to be too dependent on money? Or career success? Or on the good opinion of others?

Is the sympathy I show to others who are in trouble equal to the pity I would expend on myself if the same things happened to me?

  Let my answer before you be truthful, O God.

Create in me a pure heart, O God; and put a new and right spirit within me. Through Jesus Christ. Amen.

O GOD, ever blessed, you have given me the night for rest and the day for work and service. Grant that the refreshment from last night's sleep may now be used for your greater glory in the life of the day ahead. Do not let it produce laziness in me, but instead let it encourage more diligent action and willing obedience.

Teach me, O God, to use all the circumstances of my life today to nurture the fruits of the Spirit rather than the fruits of sin.

Let me use disappointment as material for patience;
Let me use success as material for thankfulness;
Let me use anxiety as material for perseverance;
Let me use danger as material for courage;
Let me use criticism as material for learning;
Let me use praise as material for humility;
Let me use pleasures as material for self-control;
Let me use pain as material for endurance.

O Lord Jesus Christ, for the sake of the joy that lay ahead, you endured the cross, despising its shame, and are now seated at the right hand of God; help me to think of you, who endured such opposition from sinners, so that I may not be weary and faint in my mind.

> *But that toil shall make thee*
> *Some day all Mine own,*
> *And the end of sorrow*
> *Shall be near My throne.*

Holy God, I remember before you all my friends and family, especially ___ and ___, asking that in your great love you would keep them free from sin, guiding all their deeds today in accordance with your most perfect will. Amen.

*T*o you, O heavenly Father, be all praise and glory, as day by day you richly fill my life with many blessings:

A home to share, family to love, and friends to cherish;
A place to fill and work to do;
Your gift of a green world, blue skies above, and the air we breathe;
Healthy exercise and simple pleasures;
Humanity's long history to remember and its great people to follow;
Good books to read and many creative activities to delight in;
So much that is worth knowing and the skill and technology to know it;
Thoughts of eternity and great things that sometimes fill my mind;
Many happy days, and that inward calm that you give me in days of gloom;
The peace, passing understanding, that comes from your living in me;
The faith that looks through death, and the hope of a larger life beyond the grave.

O Lord God, thank you that although you have always generously showered all people with blessings, yet in Jesus you have done greater things for us than you have ever done before:

Making home sweeter and friends dearer;
Turning sorrow into gladness and pain into the soul's victory;
Robbing death of its sting;
Robbing sin of its power;
Renewing history;
Making peace more peaceful and joy more joyful and faith and hope more secure. Amen.

O GOD of the ages, grant that I who am the heir of all the ages may gladly learn from the heavenly wisdom which in the past you have given to your servants.

A wise man wrote:
>*The world is too much with us; late and soon,*
>*Getting and spending we lay waste our powers.*
>>O God, give me grace to learn from this word.

A wise man wrote:
>*Our wills are ours to make them thine.*
>>O God, give me grace to learn from this word.

A wise king said:
>*Nothing for me is too early or too late which is in due time for thee.*
>>O God, give me grace to learn from this word.

A wise man said:
>*Expect great things from God, attempt great things for God.*
>>O God, give me grace to learn from this word.

A wise man said:
>*In his will is our peace.*
>>O God, give me grace to learn from this word.

A wise woman said:
>*The divine moment is the present moment.*
>>O God, give me grace to learn from this word.

A wise woman said:
>*He asks too much to whom God is not sufficient.*
>>O God, give me grace to learn from this word.

A wise man prayed:
>*Give what thou commandest, and command what thou wilt.*
>>O God, give me grace to pray this prayer.

A wise man prayed:
>*My past life hide; my future guide.*
>>O God, give me grace to pray this prayer.

Father, grant that in everything I do today I may remember the great traditions that I inherit, and the great cloud of witnesses that always surrounds me, so that I may be kept from doing evil and be inspired to give my best for your glory. Keep me until evening in the might of Jesus Christ my Lord. Amen.

*H*OLY God, I have dedicated my soul and life to you, yet I lament before you that I am still so inclined to sin and so reluctant to obey:

So attached to what makes me feel good, so neglectful of spiritual things;
So quick to gratify my body, so slow to nourish my soul;
So greedy for present delight, so indifferent to lasting blessing;
So fond of being lazy, so unprepared to work;
So soon at play, so delayed at prayer;
So quick to look after myself, so slow to look after others;
So eager to get, so reluctant to give;
So confident in my claims, so low in my performance;
So full of good intentions, so unwilling to fulfill them;
So harsh with those around me, so indulgent with myself;
So eager to find fault, so resentful when others find fault with me;
So unfit for great tasks, so unhappy with small ones;
So helpless without you, and yet so unwilling to be tied to you.

O merciful God, forgive me yet again. Hear this sad account of my failings and in your great mercy blot it out of your memory. Give me faith to lay hold of your perfect holiness and to rejoice in the righteousness of Christ my Savior. Grant that resting on his goodness and not my own I may become more like him, so that my will may be united with his, in obedience to yours. All this I ask for his holy name's sake. Amen.

O LORD, it is you who have given me the gift of this day's life. Give me also, I pray, the spirit to use it as I should. May I not stain the brightness of the morning with any evil thought or darken the afternoon with any shameful action. Today, let your Holy Spirit breathe into my heart clean and true desires worthy of your reign. May your truth inspire my mind. May your justice and goodness make a throne within me and direct my wayward will. May Christ be formed in me and let me learn from him how to be humble in heart, gentle in bearing, modest in speech, helpful in action, and prompt at carrying out my Father's will.

O Lord, you encompass the whole earth with your most compassionate love, and it is against your will that any of your children should be lost or die. Grant your blessing today to all who are striving to make a better world. I pray, O God, especially—

for all who are working for laws to be more just, humane, and
  transparent;
for all who are working for peace between the nations;
for all who are working to heal and prevent disease;
for all who are helping to relieve poverty;
for all who are helping the betrayed and abused;
for all who are working toward the restoration of the broken unity
  of your holy Church;
for all who preach the gospel;
for all who bear witness to Christ in every land and culture.

Break down, O Lord, all the forces of violence, cruelty, and evil. Defeat all selfish and power-driven schemes and bless everything that is planned in the spirit of Christ and carried out to the honor of his blessed name. Amen.

*G*RACIOUS GOD, as the day ends I come, seeking you. I cry out to you to create a little pool of heavenly peace in my heart as I lie down to sleep. I want to let go of the busyness, noise, and worries of today, so that my heart and mind can be still as I wait expectantly for you and meditate on your love.

Dear Father, give me tonight a deeper sense of gratitude for all your gracious gifts. Your goodness to me has been wonderful. At every moment you have cared for me and there was not a split second when I had to stand by my strength alone. When I was too preoccupied to think about you, you—though you hold the whole universe in your hands—were not too preoccupied to remember me.

O God, I am bitterly ashamed that I have to keep confessing how I forget you, how feebly I love you, and how capricious and spiritless my desire is for you. How many of your clear commandments I have disobeyed today! How many times I have held back kindness and care from you, Jesus, by not showing it to the least of your brothers and sisters whom I have encountered today!

Dear Lord, if I were to think only about the sorry state of my own heart and conscience and the good things that I did not do today, I would not have any peace before I sleep, only bitterness and despair. Therefore, dear Father, I choose instead to think of you and to be glad that your love blots out all of my sins. Loving Jesus, I choose to think of you, the Lamb of God, and to trust in your perfect righteousness. I cannot trust my own efforts nor take pleasure in what I am, but only in what you are, and what you have suffered in my place. O Holy Spirit, make my heart and mind an instrument of your work, so that as the days go by I may become more like Jesus Christ my Lord, to whom be glory forever and ever. Amen.

O MOST gracious God, grant that in everything that happens today I may carry with me the remembrance of the sufferings and death of Jesus Christ my Lord.

For your fatherly love shown in Jesus Christ your beloved Son;
For his readiness to suffer for us;
For the redemptive passion that filled his heart;
> I praise and bless your holy name.

For the power of his cross in the history of the world since he came;
For all who have taken up their own crosses and followed him;
For the noble company of martyrs and for all who are willing to die that others may live;
For all those who freely choose to suffer for the sake of others, for pain bravely endured, for sorrows of this life that have been used for the building up of eternal joys;
> I praise and bless your holy name.

O Lord my God, you dwell in pure and blessed serenity beyond the reach of human pain, and yet you look down in unspeakable love and tenderness upon the sorrows of Earth. Give me grace, I pray, to understand the meaning of the pain and disappointments that I am called to endure. Save me from worrying. Give me a strong heart to bear my own burdens. Give me a willing heart to bear the burdens of others. Give me a believing heart to cast all my burdens on you.

Glory be to you, O Father, and to you, O Christ, and to you, O Holy Spirit, forever and ever. Amen.

> *I falter where I firmly trod,*
> *And falling with my weight of cares*
> *Upon the great world's altar-stairs*
> *That slope thro' darkness up to God,*
> *I stretch lame hands of faith and grope . . .*

*E*TERNAL God, you have been the hope and joy of many generations, and in all ages you have given women and men the power to seek you, and in seeking, find you. Grant me, I pray, a clearer vision of your truth, a greater faith in your power, and a more confident assurance of your love.

When the way seems dark before me, give me grace to walk trustingly;
When so much is obscure to me, may I be all the more faithful to the little I can clearly see;
When the distant scene is clouded, may I rejoice that at least I can see the next step;
When what you are is hidden from my eyes, let me hold fast to what you command;
When I do not understand, may I remain obedient;
What I lack in faith, may I make up for in love.

O infinite God, the brightness of your face is often covered from my human gaze. Thank you for sending your Son, Jesus Christ, to be a light in a dark world. O Christ, you are the Light of Light; thank you that in your most holy life you pierced the eternal mystery, as with a great beam of heavenly light, so that in seeing you, we see the One whom no human being has ever seen.

And if I still cannot find you, O God, then let me search my heart and know whether it is I who am blind rather than you who are hidden; whether it is I who am running away from you rather than you from me. Help me to confess my sins before you, and seek your forgiveness in Jesus Christ my Lord. Amen.

O LORD my God, may I go out now to the work of another day, still surrounded by your wonderful loving kindnesses, still committed to your loyal service, still standing in your strength and not my own.

> May I today be a Christian not only in my words but also in my deeds;
> May I follow bravely in the footsteps of my Master, wherever they may lead;
> May I be uncompromising and honest with myself;
> May there be no self-pity or self-indulgence in my life today;
> May my thinking be clear, my speech truthful and open, and my action courageous and decisive.

O Lord, I pray not only for myself but for the entire community to which I belong: for all my family, friends, and colleagues, asking you to keep a fatherly eye upon them. I pray also—

> for all who today will face any great decision;
> for all those today working to settle important affairs in the lives of individuals and nations;
> for all who are shaping public opinion in our time;
> for all who write what other people read;
> for all who are lifting up the light of truth in a world of ignorance and sin;
> for all whose hands are worn with too much work, and for the unemployed whose hands have found no work today.

O Christ my Lord, who for the sake of all my brothers and sisters relinquished earthly comfort and satisfaction, forbid it that I should ever again live for myself alone. Amen.

O UNAPPROACHABLE Light, how can I raise these guilty hands to you? How can I pray to you with lips that have spoken hollow and grumpy words?

A heart hardened with vindictive passions;
An unruly tongue;
An irritable nature;
An unwillingness to bear the burdens of others;
An undue willingness to let others bear my burdens;
Exaggerated boasting about small achievements;
Fine words hiding unworthy thoughts;
A friendly face masking a cold heart;
Many neglected opportunities and many undeveloped talents;
Much love and beauty unappreciated and many blessings
    unacknowledged:
        All these I confess to you, O God.

Thank you, O loving Father, that holy and transcendent as you are, you have always shown yourself to be accessible to the prayers of sinful people like me. Especially I praise your name that in the gospel of Jesus Christ you have opened up a new and living way into your presence, making your mercy free to all who have nothing else to plead. Let me now find peace in my heart by turning away from myself and taking refuge in you. Let my despair over my miserable sins give way to joy in your adorable goodness. Let depression of mind make way for a renewed energy and a serving spirit. So let me lie down tonight thinking not of myself and my own concerns, or of my hopes and fears, or even of the ways in which I have offended you, but of others who need your help and of the work that I can do for their sakes in the vineyard of your world. Amen.

*A*LMIGHTY and most merciful Father, your power and love eternally work together for the protection of your children. Give me grace today to put my trust in you.

O Father, I pray—

for faith to believe that you rule the world in truth, justice, and love;

for faith to believe that if I seek first your kingdom and righteousness, you will provide for my needs;

for faith not to be anxious about tomorrow, but to believe that the love you have given me in the past will continue into the future;

for faith to see your loving purposes unfold in all that is happening in our time;

for faith to be calm and brave in the face of any dangers I may meet with while doing my duty;

for faith to believe in the power of your love to melt my hard heart and totally remove my sin;

for faith to put my own trust in love rather than in force, when other people harden their hearts against me;

for faith to believe in the ultimate victory of your Holy Spirit over disease and death and all the powers of darkness;

for faith to learn from any sufferings that you call me to endure;

for faith to leave in your hands the welfare of all my dear ones, especially ___ and ___.

O Lord, all my ancestors were justified in their trust in you. Rid my heart of all pointless anxieties and paralyzing fears. Give me a cheerful and buoyant spirit, and peace in doing your will; for Christ's sake. Amen.

O GOD, immortal, eternal, invisible, I remember with joy and thanksgiving all that you have been to us:

Companion of the brave;
Supporter of the loyal;
Light of the wanderer;
Joy of the pilgrim;
Guide of the pioneer;
Helper of all whose work is heavy;
Refuge of the brokenhearted;
Deliverer of the oppressed;
Relief of the tempted;
Strength of the victorious;
Ruler of rulers;
Friend of the poor;
Rescuer of the perishing;
Hope of the dying.

Give me faith now to believe that you can be all in all to me, according to my need, if only I renounce all proud self-dependence and put my trust in you.

Forbid it, O Father, that the sheer difficulty of honoring you in my life should ever tempt me to despair or give up trying. May I always keep in my mind that this human life was once divinely lived; that this world was once nobly overcome; and that this physical body, which so sorely troubles me now, was once made into your perfect dwelling place.

Show your loving kindness tonight, O Lord, to all who are in need of your help. Be with the weak to make them strong and with the strong to make them gentle. Cheer the lonely with your company and the distracted with your solitude. Prosper your Church in the fulfillment of its mighty task, and grant your blessing to all who have worked hard today in Christ's name. Amen.

CREATOR Spirit, who forever hovers over the lands and waters of earth, enriching them with forms and colors that no human skill can copy, give me today the mind and heart to rejoice in your creation.

Forbid that I should walk through your beautiful world with
    unseeing eyes;
Forbid that the attractions of the city and its shops should ever
    steal my heart away from the love of open fields and green trees;
Forbid that under the low ceiling of office or classroom or work-
    shop or study I should ever forget your great overarching sky;
Forbid that when all your creatures greet the morning with songs
    and shouts of joy, I alone should wear a grumpy and sullen
    face;
Let the energy and vigor which in your wisdom you have infused
    into every living thing stir within my being today, so that I may
    not be a lazy or mindless bystander among your creatures;
And above all give me grace to use these beauties of earth around
    me and this eager stirring of life within me to lift my soul from
    creature to Creator, and from nature to nature's God.

O Lord, your divine tenderness always outsoars the narrow loves and kindnesses of earth. Grant me today a kind and gentle heart toward all things that live. Help me to take a stand against cruelty to any creatures of yours. Help me to be actively concerned for the welfare of little children, and those who are sick, and of the poor, remembering that what I do for the least of these brothers and sisters of his, I do for Jesus Christ my Lord. Amen.

*A*LMIGHTY and blessed God, you have never left yourself without a witness on earth. In every age you have raised up holy and prophetic people to lead us into the way of faith and love. I praise your name for the gift of your holy apostle Saint Paul. Thank you for the zeal you gave him to carry the lamp of truth, already lit in the East, into the Western world.

> Saint Paul said, *Put away from you all bitterness and wrath and anger and wrangling and slander, together with all malice, and be kind to one another, tenderhearted, forgiving one another, as God in Christ has forgiven you.*
> O God, incline my heart to follow in this way.
> Saint Paul said, *Put on the Lord Jesus Christ, and make no provision for the flesh, to gratify its desires.*
> O God, incline my heart to follow in this way.
> Saint Paul said, *I beat my body and make it my slave so that after I have preached to others, I myself will not be disqualified for the prize.*
> O God, incline my heart to follow in this way.
> Saint Paul said, *Do nothing from selfish ambition or conceit, but in humility regard others as better than yourselves.*
> O God, incline my heart to follow in this way.
> Saint Paul said, *Let the one who boasts, boast in the Lord.*
> O God, incline my heart to follow in this way.
> Saint Paul said, *Devote yourselves to prayer, keeping alert in it with thanksgiving. At the same time pray for us as well that God will open to us a door for the word, that we may declare the mystery of Christ . . .*

O God, I pray tonight especially for all who, following in the footsteps of Saint Paul, are crossing frontiers to share the light of Christ's gospel. Amen.

*G*LORY to you, O Lord my King! In love and awe I greet you at the beginning of another day! I give you all my praise and love and loyalty, O Lord most high!

Help me, O Lord God, not to let my thoughts today be wholly occupied by the world's passing show. In your loving kindness you have given me the power to lift my mind to contemplate the unseen and eternal; help me not to remain content only with what I see and feel, here and now. Instead grant that each day may do something to strengthen my grasp of the unseen world and my sense of the reality of that world. And so, as the end of my earthly life draws ever nearer, bind my heart to the holy interests of that unseen world, so that I may not grow to be a part of these fleeting earthly surroundings, but instead grow more and more ready for the life of the world to come.

O Lord, you see and know all things. Give me grace, I pray, to know you so well and to see you so clearly that in knowing you I may know myself as completely as you know me; and in seeing you I may see myself as I really am before you. Give me today a clear vision of my life in time as it appears in your eternity. Show me my own smallness and your infinite greatness. Show me my own sin and your perfect righteousness. Show me my own lack of love and your exceeding love. Yet in your mercy show me also how, small as I am, I can take refuge in your greatness; how, sinful as I am, I may lean upon your righteousness; and how, loveless as I am, I may hide myself in your forgiving love. Help me today to keep my thoughts centered on the life and death of Jesus Christ my Lord, so that I may see all things in the light of the redemption which you have granted to me in his name. Amen.

O LORD, you are the Lord of the night as you are of the day, and all the stars are obedient to your will. In this hour of darkness, I too submit my will to yours.

O God, set me free—

from the stirrings of self will within my heart;
from cowardly avoidance of the things I need to do;
from rebellious reluctance to face necessary suffering;
from discontentment with my place in life;
from jealousy of those whose place in life is easier;
from being dissatisfied with my talents yet hungry for more;
from the pride which sets human knowledge above your wisdom;
from undisciplined thought;
from being unwilling to learn and disinclined to serve.

O God my Father, you are often closest to me when I am farthest from you, and you are near at hand even when I feel that you have abandoned me; mercifully grant that the defeat of my self-centeredness may be the triumph in me of your eternal purpose.

May I grow more sure of your reality and power;
May I reach a clearer picture of the meaning of my life on Earth;
May I strengthen my hold on eternal life;
May I look increasingly to what lies beyond my vision;
May my desires become less unruly and my thoughts more pure;
May my love for other people grow deeper and more tender, and
    may I be more willing to take their burdens upon myself.

To your care, O God, I commend my soul and the souls of all whom I love and who love me; through Jesus Christ our Lord. Amen.

SUNDAY MORNING

SUNDAY MORNING

*H*oly, Holy, Holy, Lord God Almighty; heaven and earth are full of your glory; glory be to you, O Lord most high.

O God, I ask for your blessing on this day of rest and refreshment. Let me rejoice today in your worship and be glad as I sing your praise. Do not let me concentrate today on the refreshment of my body rather than my spirit. Let my spirit be refreshed today as well as my body. Give me grace to gather myself together and center my heart on you. Help me to step aside for a little while from the busyness of life and think about its meaning and its end. Today, may Jesus Christ be the companion of my thoughts so that his divine humanity may take deeper root within my soul. May he be in me and I in him, just as you, Father, were in him, and through him may be in me; and so I may rest in you.

O Lord, you are the source and ground of all truth, the Light of Lights. You have opened the minds of men and women to understand the world and its secrets; guide me in the time I spend reading today. Give me grace to choose the right books and to read them in the right way. Give me wisdom to be selective, as well as strength to persevere. Let the Bible have its rightful place, and grant that as I read I may be alive to the stirrings of your Holy Spirit in my soul.

I pray, O God, for all those who are seeking you earnestly today, and for every group of men and women who are meeting together to praise and magnify your name. Whatever their way of worship, I ask you in your love to accept their sincere offering of prayers and praise, and lead them into life eternal; through Jesus Christ our Lord. Amen.

SUNDAY EVENING

*H*OLY Spirit of God, you are a gracious and willing guest in every heart that is humble enough to receive you. Be present now within my heart and guide my prayer.

For all the gracious opportunities and privileges of this day, I give you thanks, O Lord;

For the rest I have enjoyed today from work and chores;
For your invitation to keep this day holy for you;
For church and the ministry of public worship;
For the blessed sacrament in which, as often as we eat and drink it, we remember our Lord's death and taste his living presence;
For all the physical symbols through which heavenly realities have today grasped my soul more firmly;
For the books I have read and the music which has lifted my heart;
For today's friendly conversations;
For the Sabbath peace of Christian homes;
For the inner peace which has ruled within my heart.

Grant, O heavenly Father, that the spiritual renewal I have enjoyed today may not be left behind and forgotten as tomorrow I return to the daily cycle of work. Here is a fountain of inward strength. Here is a purifying wind that will blow through all the business, work, and relaxation of the coming week. Here is light to illuminate my road. Therefore, O God, help me to discipline my will so that in hours of stress I may honestly seek after those things which I have prayed for in hours of peace.

Before I lie down to sleep, I commit all my dear ones to your unsleeping care; through Jesus Christ our Lord. Amen.

Acknowledgments

*I*n addition to those mentioned in the preface to the new edition, I would also like to acknowledge and thank:

God—you have been my refuge and my strength at all times.

My husband, Stu, and our children—for their unfailing support and love.

Scribner—for their support and enthusiasm for this project.

Bishop Julian Henderson—through whom *A Diary of Private Prayer* first came to me.

My family and friends who have prayed for this new edition with me over the years: the Millers, Jourdains, Woollgars, Wrights, Hunts, Hobleys, and Munns, and Deborah Andrews, Rebecca Daynes, Anna Farrell, and Heather Grizzle. Your prayers have meant so much.

Anna Thayer and Esther Woollgar—for help in the early days.

Mark Batterson—whose book inspired me to circle this project in prayer.

Those who have kindly endorsed this new edition.

I dedicate my work in this new edition to my children, Jed and Lily; keep praying and never give up!

Notes

*A*ll biblical quotes are taken from the New Revised Standard Version (NRSV) of the Bible, unless otherwise noted.

First Day, Evening
My soul is satisfied: Psalm 63:5–6.

Second Day, Evening
Create in me a clean heart: Psalm 5:10–12.

Third Day, Evening
Whom have I in heaven: Psalm 73:25.

Fifth Day, Morning
This poor soul called: Psalm 34:6.

Fifth Day, Evening
Though earth and man were gone: Emily Brontë (1818–48), "No Coward Soul Is Mine."

Sixth Day, Evening
But not yet: Saint Augustine, *Confessions.*

Eighth Day, Morning
Whenever you stand praying: Mark 11:25.
It is more blessed: Acts 20:35.
When you give alms: Matthew 6:3.
Enter through the narrow gate: Matthew 7:13.
Do not judge: Matthew 7:1.

Tenth Day, Morning
O God, you are my God: Psalm 63:1–3.
Seven times a day: Psalm 119:164–65.

How can young people: Psalm 119:9.
Make me to know your ways: Psalm 25:4–5.
Set a guard over my mouth: Psalm 141:3.
Keep my steps steady: Psalm 119:133.
O Lord, who may abide: Psalm 15:1–5.
Let the words of my mouth: Psalm 19:14.

Eleventh Day, Morning
What are you doing: Matthew 5:47.

Twelfth Day, Evening
And Thou, O Lord: John Greenleaf Whittier (1807–82), "The Eternal Goodness."

Fourteenth Day, Evening
Here I am: Isaiah 6:8.

Sixteenth Day, Morning
My soul yearns for you: Isaiah 26:9.
I steadier step: Arthur Hugh Clough (1819–61), "It Fortifies My Soul to Know."

Sixteenth Day, Evening
all of them deserted him: Mark 14:50.
My God, My God: Mark 15:34.
We may not know: Cecil Frances Alexander (1823–95), "There Is a Green Hill."

Eighteenth Day, Morning
Do not store up: Matthew 6:19–20.
Stive first for the kingdom: Matthew 6:33.
Do good: Luke 6:35.
Love your enemies: Luke 6:35.
Do not fear: Luke 8:50.
Unless you change: Matthew 18:3.
Ask, and it will be given: Matthew 7:7.

Eighteenth Day, Evening
If we say that we have: 1 John 1:8.

Twentieth Day, Evening
I call upon you: Psalm 141:1–2.
O Lord, open my lips: Psalm 51:15.
Bless the Lord: Psalm 103:2–5.
But who can detect: Psalm 19:12–13.
Have mercy on me: Psalm 51:1–3.
Be to me a rock: Psalm 31:2–3.
I will both lie down: Psalm 4:8.

Twenty-first Day, Morning
My heart an altar: George Croly (1780–1860), "Spirit of God, Descend upon My Heart."

Twenty-first Day, Evening
For here we have no lasting city: Hebrews 13:14.

Twenty-third Day, Evening
Create in me a pure heart: Psalm 51:10.

Twenty-fourth Day, Morning
But that toil shall make thee: Seventh-century hymn by Andrew of Crete, translated by John M. Neale (1818–66).

Twenty-fifth Day, Morning
The world is too much with us: William Wordsworth (1770–1850), "The World Is Too Much With Us."
Our wills are ours: Alfred, Lord Tennyson (1809–92), "In Memoriam A. H. H."
Nothing for me is too early: Marcus Aurelius, *Meditations*.
Expect great things from God: William Carey (1761–1834), "The Deathless Sermon."
In his will is our peace: Dante Alighieri, *Paradiso*.
The divine moment: Saint Catherine of Siena.
He asks too much: Unknown.
Give what thou commandest: Saint Augustine, *Confessions*.

Twenty-seventh Day, Evening
I falter where I firmly trod: Alfred, Lord Tennyson, "In Memoriam A. H. H."

Thirtieth Day, Evening
Put away from you: Ephesians 4:31–32.
put on the Lord Jesus Christ: Romans 13:14.
I beat my body: 1 Corinthians 9:27 (NIV translation).
Do nothing from selfish ambition: Philippians 2:3.
Let the one who boasts: I Corinthians 1:31.
Devote yourselves to prayer: Colossians 4:2.